Eye Candy for Andy

poems by

John J. Trause

Finishing Line Press
Georgetown, Kentucky

Eye Candy for Andy

*This book is dedicated to all the luminaries
whose light shined in the darkness of the Factory.*

ACKNOWLEDGMENTS

I thank the editors and publishers of these publications in which some of the
poetry in this collection has appeared before.

The poems in *Eye Candy for Andy* appeared as "13 Most Beautiful…: Poems
for Andy Warhol's Screen Tests" in *A Glorious Wild-Winged Adventure in
Writing: An anthology of their collected works* [Wild Angels Poets and Writers
Group] issue 10 (spring 2010) and in *ditch* [online Saturday, August 22, 2009].

Publisher: Leah Huete de Maines
Editor: Christen Kincaid
Cover Art: Eddie Rivera and John J. Trause. Photograph by Jill Greenberg.
Interior Art: Galen Warden
Author Photo: Michaelangelo Di Nonno
Cover Design: Elizabeth Maines McCleavy

Order online: www.finishinglinepress.com
also available on amazon.com

Author inquiries and mail orders:
Finishing Line Press
PO Box 1626
Georgetown, Kentucky 40324
USA

Table of Contents

Between 1964 and 1966 artist, filmmaker, and master of appropriation Andy Warhol shot nearly 500 Screen Tests, modeled in his own way on the Hollywood practice. The result is a collection of moving portrait of hundreds of different individuals, from celebrities to the less well-known, who happen to be visitors to the Factory, the name given to his studio. Using a stationary film camera (16 mm Bolex) and a strong key light, Warhol brought out the personalities of his subjects in beautifully revealing ways. Each Screen Test was shot on silent, black-and-white, 100-foot rolls of film, creating two-and-a-half-minute film reels to be screened in slow motion (four minutes each). A cross between still and moving image, various assortments of these mini-masterpieces were grouped to form longer films, including *13 Most Beautiful Women* (1964) and *13 Most Beautiful Boys* (1964).

Commissioned in 2008 by the Andy Warhol Museum and the Pittsburgh Cultural Trust to score a selection of thirteen of the Screen Tests, musicians Dean Wareham and Britta Phillips, formerly of the band Luna and currently appearing as Dean & Britta, created new soundtracks for the thirteen films, incorporating original compositions as well as cover songs. They sorted through Warhol's films, made a selection of iconic subjects, and produced 13 Most Beautiful... Songs for Andy Warhol's Screen Tests, a multimedia show, which they have had on tour ever since.

The 13 Screen Tests included are Ann Buchanan, Paul America, Edie Sedgwick, Billy Name, Susan Bottomly, Dennis Hopper, Mary Woronov, Nico, Freddy Herko, Richard Rheem, Ingrid Superstar, Lou Reed (Coke), and Jane Holzer (Toothbrush).

Ann Buchanan

A tear rolls
down
from
her right eye   her left eye
and in a beat
lands on
her chin.

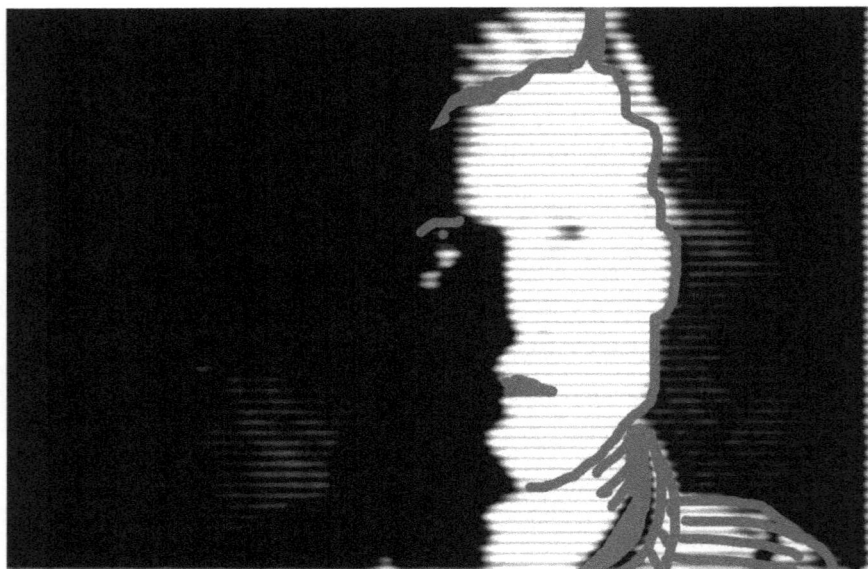

Paul America

You can chew
on me
for four minutes
too.

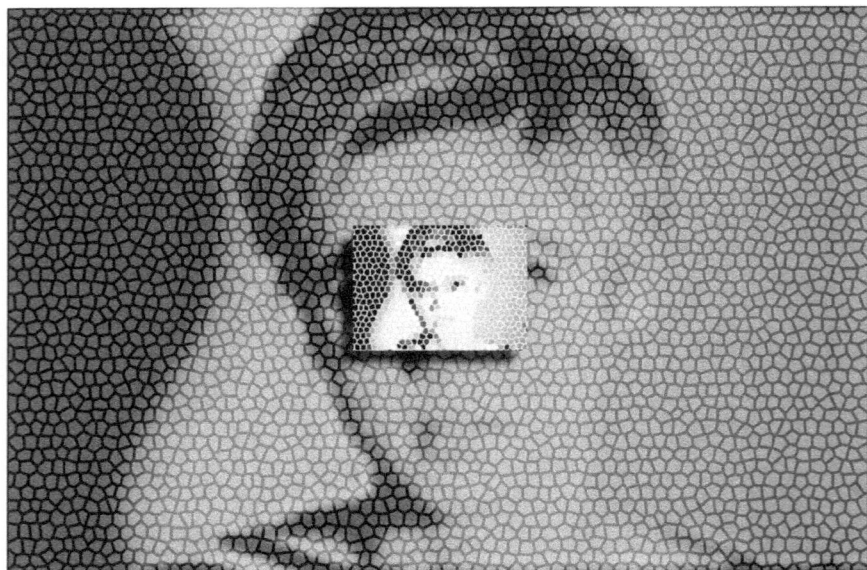

Edie Sedgwick

If not silver,
burnt sienna.

****

I wish they all could be
Callie-pornia girls.

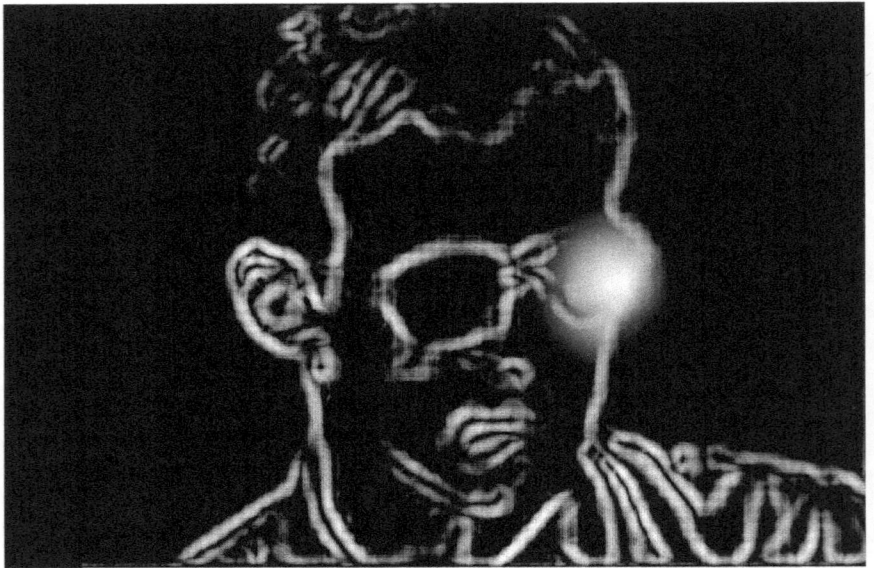

Billy Name

Lighting by Billy
Lit by Billy
Lining by Billy
Silver by Billy,
and what's in a name?
With eyes disguised,
named by Billy.

Susan Bottomly

The bottom left
of her face
is left.
That's right.

Dennis Hopper

Trading in his
leopard-skin loincloth
for a herringbone tweed blazer
Tarzan gazes gorgeously.

Mary Woronov

Slackening
near-palindrome
swimming underground
smirks, smiles,
a sphinx.

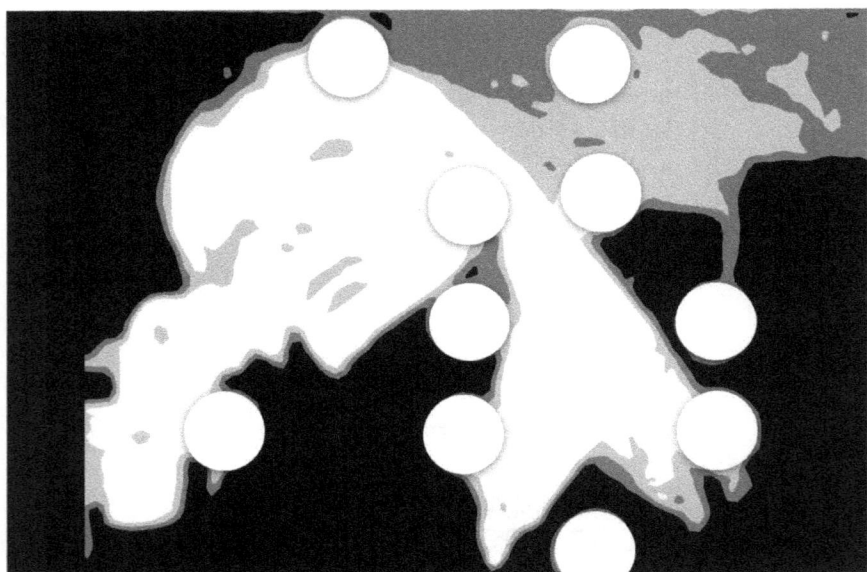

Nico

There are worse
sins than nicotine:
nicophilia
nicomania
nicolatria
nicodulia
nicosis.
And she nictates
and takes dictation.

Freddy Herko

Before he danced himself
to the end of love,
he had his last cigarette,
another window of opportunity.

Richard Rheem

California: 26 gasoline stations
New York City: 26 husbands
13 most beautiful…
13 most beautiful…

Ingrid Superstar

Blondie (another)
from New Jersey
chokes back tears,
another blonde on
the Factory production line.

Lou Reed

With eyes disguised
one pop icon
drinks another
pop.

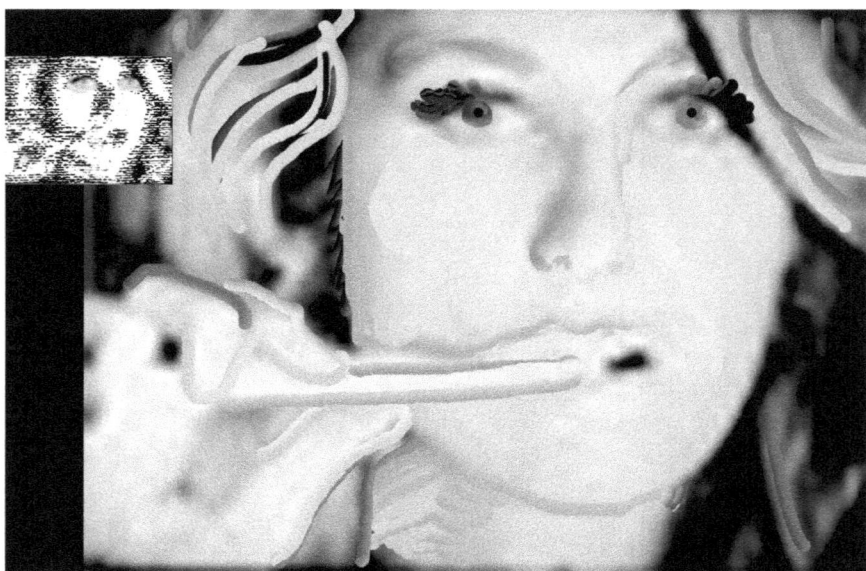

Baby Jane Holzer

Me brush long time.

JOHN J. TRAUSE, said to be the secret love child of Henri Langlois and Mary Meerson (Or is it Marie Menken and Willard Maas?), is the Director of Oradell Public Library and the author most recently of *Why Sing?* (Sensitive Skin Press, 2017), a book of traditional and experimental poems; *Picture This: For Your Eyes and Ears* (Dos Madres Press, 2016), a book of poems on art, film, and photography; Exercises in High Treason (great weather for MEDIA, 2016), a book of fictive translations, found poems, and manipulated texts; *Inside Out, Upside Down, and Round and Round* (Nirala Publications, 2012); *Seriously Serial* (Poets Wear Prada, 2007; rev. ed. 2014); and *Latter-Day Litany* (Éditions élastiques, 1996), the latter staged Off Broadway. His translations, poetry, prose, scholarship, and visual work appear internationally in many journals and anthologies, including the artists' periodical *Crossings*, the Dada journal *Maintenant*, the experimental art and literary journal *Offerta Speciale*, the Uphook Press anthologies *Hell Strung and Crooked* and *-gape-seed-*, the Great Weather for Media anthologies *It's Animal but Merciful* (2012), *I Let Go of the Stars in My Hand* (2014), *Birds Fall Silent in the Mechanical Sea* (2019), *Paper Teller Diorama* (2021), *A Shape Produced by a Curve* (2023), and *Rabbit Ears: TV Poems* (NYQ Books, 2015). Marymark Press has published his visual poetry and art as broadsides and sheets. He is the subject of a 30-on-30-in-30 essay on The Operating System, written by Don Zirilli, and an author of an essay on Baroness Elsa at the same site, both in April 2016. He has shared the stage with Steven Van Zandt, Anne Waldman, Karen Finley, Andrei Codrescu, and Jerome Rothenberg; the page with Billy Collins, Lita Hornick, William Carlos Williams, Woody Allen, Ted Kooser, Victor Buono, and Pope John Paul II; and the cage with the Cumaean Sibyl, Ezra Pound, Hannibal Lector, Andrei Chikatilo, and George "The Animal" Steele. He is a co-founder of the William Carlos Williams Poetry Cooperative (The Red Wheelbarrow) in Rutherford, N. J., and former host of its monthly reading series. His artwork has been exhibited in The Museum of Modern Art Staff Show (1995), at Il Trapezio Café (Nutley, N.J.), and in the permanent collection of The Museum of Menstruation (New Carrollton, Md.) to whose website he has contributed. For the sake of art he hung naked for one whole month in the summer of 2007 on the Art Wall of the Bowery Poetry Club. He is fond of cunning acrostics and color-coded chiasmus.